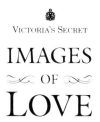

Victoria's Secret

IMAGES
OF
LOVE

IMAGES

∽◦∽ OF ∽◦∽

LOVE

VOLUME TWO

Authorized Purveyors

VICTORIA'S SECRET

Nº 10 MARGARET STREET
LONDON W1

WEIDENFELD & NICOLSON

LONDON

IN THIS, THE SECOND anthology of love, I have taken more of my favourite pieces of verse and prose, and have matched them with images of equal beauty and romance to create another treasury of words and pictures on the theme of love's infinite variety.

Every lover will recognize the tremulous uncertainties of first love depicted here, the simple longing expressed anonymously in a Victorian valentine, the glow of happiness felt by Elizabeth Bennett in the knowledge of her love, and Tess of the d'Urbervilles' profound and speechless joy. No woman can ever have received more tender expressions of love than Fanny Brawne from John Keats, or more seductive persuasion than Teresa Guiccioli from Lord Byron; and no man can ever have received a more heartfelt and moving declaration of devotion than Anne Bradstreet's husband three centuries ago.

In the ever-changing, fleeting world of love, such solemn and rapturous celebrations of love fulfilled may find their match in wistful meditations on love lost or altered; and even the most romantic love must sometimes come to an end, finding its last expression in heartrending farewells, sometimes bitterly reproachful, sometimes sweetly melancholy.

I have paired all the pieces in these pages – whether bashful confessions or urgent pleas, ecstatic celebrations or poignant adieus – with images which not only reflect them in mood and content, but also add a further dimension to the intensity and beauty of the words. Together they mirror something of the mystery, the subtlety and the sheer power of love; for, as William Morris wrote, lovers inhabit a world apart, where 'love is enough':

Though the hills be held shadows, and the sea a dark wonder,
    And this day draw a veil over all deeds pass'd over,
Yet their hands shall not tremble, their feet shall not falter:
The void shall not weary, the fear shall not alter
    These lips and the eyes of the loved and the lover.

With Love

MARRIAGE MORNING

Light, so low upon earth,
    You send a flash to the sun.
Here is the golden close of love,
    All my wooing is done.
Oh, the woods and the meadows,
    Woods where we hid from the wet,
Stiles where we stay'd to be kind,
    Meadows in which we met!

Light, so low in the vale
    You flash and lighten afar,
For this is the golden morning of love,
    And you are his morning star.
Flash, I am coming, I come,
    By meadow and stile and wood,
Oh, lighten into my eyes and heart,
    Into my heart and my blood!

Heart, are you great enough
    For a love that never tires?
O heart, are you great enough for love?
    I have heard of thorns and briers.
Over the thorns and briers,
    Over the meadows and stiles,
Over the world to the end of it
    Flash for a million miles.

ALFRED, LORD TENNYSON 1809–92

*S*O SWEET LOVE SEEMED

So Sweet seemed that April morn,
When first we kissed beside the thorn
So strangely sweet, it was not strange
We thought that love never could change.
But I can tell – let the truth be told –
That love will change in growing old;
Though day by day is nought to see,
So delicate his motions be.
His little spring, that sweet we found,
So deep in summer floods is drowned
I wonder, bathed in joy complete,
How love so young could be so sweet.

ROBERT BRIDGES 1844–1930

PROUD WORD YOU NEVER SPOKE

Proud word you never spoke, but you will speak
Four not exempt from pride some future day.
Resting on one white hand a warm wet cheek,
    Over my open volume you will say,
        'This man loved *me*' – then rise and trip away.

WALTER SAVAGE LANDOR 1775–1864

TO THE DAISY

With little here to do or see
Of things that in the great world be,
Daisy! again I talk to thee,
    For thou art worthy,
Thou unassuming Commonplace
Of Nature, with that homely face,
And yet with something of a grace
    Which love makes for thee!

Sweet Flower! for by that name at last
When all my reveries are past
I call thee, and to that cleave fast,
    Sweet silent creature!
That breath'st with me in sun and air,
Do thou, as thou art wont, repair
My heart with gladness, and a share
    Of thy meek nature!

WILLIAM WORDSWORTH 1770–1850

FORGET-ME-NOT

This little gem of azure hue,
    Is full of interest to me,
Because, my love, it tells of you,
    In silent language, clear and free.
Its modest bloom in such a spot,
    In hue it's kindred to the sky,
Confirm the sweet Forget-me-not,
    The flower of Hope and Constancy.

ANONYMOUS NINETEENTH CENTURY

JENNY KISS'D ME

Jenny kissed me when we met,
Jumping from the chair she sat in.
Time, you thief! who love to get
Sweets into your list, put that in.
Say I'm weary, say I'm sad;
Say that health and wealth have missed me;
Say I'm growing old, but add –
Jenny kissed me.

JAMES HENRY LEIGH HUNT 1784–1859

$\mathcal{L}$OVE'S POSSESSION

Men were at work here and there – for it was the season for 'taking up' the meadows, or digging the little waterways clear for the winter irrigation, and mending their banks where trodden down by the cows. Clare hardily kept his arm round her waist in sight of these watermen, with the air of a man who was accustomed to public dalliance, though actually as shy as

she who, with lips parted and eyes askance on the labourers, wore the look of a wary animal the while.

'You are not ashamed of owning me as yours before them!' she said gladly.

'Oh no!'

'But if it should reach the ears of your friends at Emminster that you are walking about like this with me, a milkmaid –'

'The most bewitching milkmaid ever seen.'

'They might feel it a hurt to their dignity.'

'My dear girl – a d'Urberville hurt the dignity of a Clare! It is a grand card to play – that of your belonging to such a family, and I am reserving it for a grand effect when we are married, and have the proofs of your descent from Parson Tringham. Apart from that, my future is to be totally foreign to my family – it will not affect even the surface of their lives. We shall leave this part of England – perhaps England itself – and what does it matter how people regard us here? You will like going, will you not?'

She could answer no more than a bare affirmative, so great was the emotion aroused in her at the thought of going through the world with him as his own familiar friend. Her feelings almost filled her ears like a babble of waves, and surged up to her eyes. She put her hand in his, and thus they went on, to a place where the reflected sun glared up from the river, under a bridge, with a molten-metallic glow that dazzled their eyes, though the sun itself was hidden by the bridge. They stood still, whereupon little furred and feathered heads popped up from the smooth surface of the water; but, finding that the disturbing presences had paused, and not passed by, they disappeared again. Upon this river-brink they lingered till the fog began to close round them – which was very early in the evening at this time of the year – settling on the lashes of her eyes, where it rested like crystals, and on his brows and hair.

Tess of the d'Urbervilles, THOMAS HARDY 1840–1928

$\mathcal{C}$ARRIER LETTER

My hands have not touched water since your hands, –
    No; – nor my lips freed laughter since 'farewell'.
And with the day, distance again expands
    Between us, voiceless as an uncoiled shell.

Yet, – much follows, much endures . . . Trust birds alone:
    A dove's wings clung about my heart last night
With surging gentleness; and the blue stone
    Set in the tryst⁄ring has but worn more bright.

HART CRANE 1899–1932

ROWING TOGETHER

Amy had been dabbling her hand in the water during the little pause that fell between them, and, when she looked up, Laurie was leaning on his oars, with an expression in his eyes that made her say hastily, merely for the sake of saying something, –

'You must be tired; rest a little, and let me row.'

'I'm not tired; but you may take an oar, if you like.'

Amy accepted. She rowed as well as she did many other things; and, though she used both hands, and Laurie but one, the oars kept time, and the boat went smoothly through the water.

'How well we pull together, don't we?' said Amy, who objected to silence just then.

'So well that I wish we might always pull in the same boat. Will you, Amy?' very tenderly.

'Yes, Laurie,' very low.

Then they both stopped rowing, and unconsciously added a pretty little *tableau* of human love and happiness to the dissolving views reflected in the lake.

Good Wives, LOUISA M. ALCOTT 1832–88

*H*IM WHO PASSIONATELY LOVED YOU

My dearest Teresa,

I have read this book in your garden; — my love, you were absent, or else I could not have read it. It is a favourite book of yours, and the writer was a friend of mine. You will not understand these English words, and *others* will not understand

them. – which is the reason I have not scrawled them in Italian. But you will recognize the handwriting of him who passionately loved you, and you will divine that, over a book which was yours, he could only think of love.

In that word, beautiful in all languages, but most so in yours – *Amor mio* – is comprised my existence here and hereafter. I feel I exist here, and I feel I shall exist hereafter, – to *what* purpose you will decide; my destiny rests with you, and you are a woman, eighteen years of age, and two out of a convent, . . .

I love you, and you love me, – at least, you *say so*, and *act* as if you *did so*, which last is a great consolation in all events. But *I* more than love you and cannot cease to love you.

Think of me, sometimes, when the Alps and ocean divide us, – but they never will, unless you *wish* it.

GEORGE GORDON, LORD BYRON 1788–1824

A VALEDICTION

If we must part,
   Then let it be like this;
Not heart on heart,
   Nor with the useless anguish of a kiss;
But touch mine hand and say;
'*Until tomorrow or some other day,*
   If we must part.'

Words are so weak
   When love hath been so strong:
Let silence speak:
'*Life is a little while, and love is long;*
A time to sow and reap,
And after harvest a long time to sleep,
But words are weak.'

ERNEST DOWSON 1867–1900

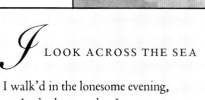

𝓘 LOOK ACROSS THE SEA

I walk'd in the lonesome evening,
    And who so sad as I,
When I saw the young men and maidens
    Merrily passing by.
        To thee, my Love, to thee –
        So fain would I come to thee!
While the ripples fold upon sands of gold
        And I look across the sea.

I stretch out my hands; who will clasp them?
    I call, – thou repliest no word:
O why should heart-longing be weaker
    Than the waving wings of a bird!
        To thee, my Love, to thee –
        So fain would I come to thee!
For the tide's at rest from east to west,
        And I look across the sea.

There's joy in the hopeful morning,
    There's peace in the parting day,
There's sorrow with every lover
    Whose true love is far away.
        To thee, my Love, to thee –
        So fain would I come to thee!
And the water's bright in a still moonlight,
        As I look across the sea.

WILLIAM ALLINGHAM 1824–89

 LOVE IN A LIFE

Room after room,
I hunt the house through
We inhabit together.
Heart, fear nothing, for, heart, thou shalt find her,
Next time, herself! – not the trouble behind her
Left in the curtain, the couch's perfume!
As she brushed it, the cornice-wreath blossomed anew:
Yon looking-glass gleamed at the wave of her feather.

Yet the day wears,
And door succeeds door;
I try the fresh fortune –
Range the wide house from the wing to the centre.
Still the same chance! she goes out as I enter.
Spend my whole day in the quest – who cares?
But 'tis twilight, you see, – with such suites to explore,
Such closets to search, such alcoves to importune!

ROBERT BROWNING 1812–89

 DECLARATION

Margaret and Mr Lennox strolled along the little terrace-walk under the south wall, where the bees still hummed and worked busily in their hives.

'What a perfect life you seem to live here! I have always felt rather contemptuously towards the poets before, with their wishes, "Mine be a cot beside a hill," and that sort of thing: but now I am afraid that the truth is, I have been nothing better than a Cockney. Just now I feel as if twenty years' hard study of law would be amply rewarded by one year of such an exquisite serene life as this – such skies!' looking up – 'such crimson and amber foliage, so perfectly motionless as that!' pointing to some of the great forest trees which shut in the garden as if it were a nest. . . .

'Margaret,' said he, taking her by surprise, and getting sudden possession of her hand, so that she was forced to stand still and listen, despising herself for the fluttering at her heart all the time; 'Margaret, I wish you did not like Helstone so much – did not seem so perfectly calm and happy here. I have been hoping for these three months past to find you regretting London – and London friends, a little – enough to make you listen more kindly' (for she was quietly, but firmly, striving to extricate her hand from his grasp) 'to one who has not much to offer, it is true – nothing but prospects in the future – but who does love you, Margaret, almost in spite of himself. Margaret, have I startled you to much? Speak!'

North and South, ELIZABETH GASKELL 1812–65

$\mathscr{F}$IRST TIME HE KISSED ME

First time he kissed me, he but only kiss'd
   The fingers of this hand wherewith I write;
   And ever since, it grew more clean and white,
Slow to world-greetings, quick with its 'Oh, list,'
When the angels speak. A ring of amethyst
   I could not wear here, plainer to my sight,
   Than that first kiss. The second pass'd in height
The first, and sought the forehead, and half miss'd,
Half falling on the hair. Oh, beyond meed!
   That was the chrism of love, which love's own crown,
With sanctifying sweetness, did precede.
   The third upon my lips was folded down
In perfect, purple state; since when, indeed,
   I have been proud, and said, 'My love, my own!'

ELIZABETH BARRETT BROWNING 1806–61

THE MUSIC OF LOVE

How oft, when thou, my music, music play'st
Upon that blessèd wood whose motion sounds
With thy sweet fingers when thou gently sway'st
The wiry concord that mine ear confounds,
Do I envy those jacks that nimble leap
To kiss the tender inward of thy hand,
Whilst my poor lips, which should that harvest reap,
At the wood's boldness by thee blushing stand.
To be so tickled, they would change their state
And situation with those dancing chips
O'er whom thy fingers walk with gentle gait,
Making dead wood more blest than living lips.
 Since saucy jacks so happy are in this,
 Give them thy fingers, me thy lips to kiss.

WILLIAM SHAKESPEARE 1564–1616

THE TALKING OAK

Say thou, whereon I carved her name,
 If ever maid or spouse,
As fair as my Olivia, came
 To rest beneath thy boughs. –

But tell me, did she read the name
 I carved with many vows
When last with throbbing heart I came
 To rest beneath thy boughs?

'O yes, she wander'd round and round
 These knotted knees of mine,
And found, and kiss'd the name she found,
 And sweetly murmur'd thine.

'A teardrop trembled from its source,
 And down my surface crept.
My sense of touch is something coarse,
 But I believe she wept.

'Then flush'd her cheek with rosy light,
 She glanced across the plain;
But not a creature was in sight:
 She kiss'd me once again.

'Her kisses were so close and kind,
 That, trust me on my word,
Hard wood I am, and wrinkled rind,
 But yet my sap was stirr'd:

'And even into my inmost ring
   A pleasure I discern'd,
Like those blind motions of the Spring,
   That show the year is turn'd.

'Thrice-happy he that may caress
   The ringlet's waving balm —
The cushions of whose touch may press
   The maiden's tender palm.

ALFRED, LORD TENNYSON 1809–92

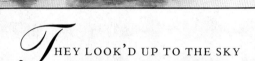

*T*HEY LOOK'D UP TO THE SKY

They look'd up to the sky, whose floating glow
   Spread like a rosy ocean, vast and bright;
They gazed upon the glittering sea below,
   Whence the broad moon rose circling into sight;

They heard the waves splash, and the wind so low,
   And saw each other's dark eyes darting light
Into each other – and, beholding this,
Their lips drew near, and clung into a kiss;

A long, long kiss, a kiss of youth, and love,
   And beauty, all concentrating like rays
Into one focus, kindled from above;
   Such kisses as belong to early days,
Where heart, and soul, and sense, in concert move,
   And the blood's lava, and the pulse a blaze,
Each kiss a heart-quake, – for a kiss's strength,
I think it must be reckon'd by its length.

GEORGE GORDON, LORD BYRON 1788–1824

A YOUNG MAN'S DESIRE

My dearest, my beautiful, will you write to me again, will you say that word which, in this last letter, you timidly avoid? I shall tremble with an exquisite happiness, if I read it written by you. Will you give me that moment of delight?

I look at your portrait. It shows one of the sweetest faces I ever saw, but your own face of today is more – beautiful, fuller of meaning. I have no words to utter the sense of worship with which I think of your pure and noble nature – legible to me in your face, audible in your voice, and expressed so plainly in your letter. Dearest, you are very far above me, and it is strange, strange, that you should care to be loved by me. And yet, I think no one could love you so profoundly as I do. We have met only twice, have written two or three times to each other – and I know you better than any other woman, I feel you are more to me than any living soul.

I will have no more doubts and fears. You, you, shall save me out of my dark cheerless life. I will live for you, work for you, think only of you, make you the whole end and purpose of my being. Dearest, dearest, I love you beyond all that I ever imagined of love. You are the incredible woman – the ideal of a passionate heart; yet you *live*, you write to me, I hear your voice as I read your letters. And I shall some day hear you *say to* me, with your very lips, what you have not yet dared to write.

May I not hope for that?

GEORGE GISSING 1857–1903

[38]

OR LOVE

How long shall I pine for love?
　　How long shall I use in vain?
How long like the turtle-dove
　　Shall I heavenly thus complain?
Shall the sails of my love stand still?
Shall the grists of my hopes be unground?
　　Oh fie, oh fie, oh fie,
　　Let the mill, let the mill go round.

JOHN FLETCHER 1579–1625

THE LATTICE WINDOW

Emily, as she approached the lattice, was sensible of the features of this scene only as they served to bring Valancourt more immediately to her fancy. 'Ah!' said she with a heavy sigh, as she threw herself into a chair by the window, 'how often have we sat together on this spot – often have looked upon that landscape! Never, never more shall we view it together! – never, never more, perhaps, shall we look upon each other!'

Her tears were suddenly stopped by terror: a voice spoke near her in the pavilion – she shrieked: it spoke again; and she distinguished the well-known tones of Valancourt. It was, indeed, Valancourt who supported her in his arms! For some moments their emotion would not suffer either to speak. 'Emily,' said Valancourt at length, as he pressed her hand in his, 'Emily!' – and he was again silent; but the accent in which

he had pronounced her name expressed all his tenderness and sorrow.

'O my Emily!' he resumed after a long pause, 'I do then see you once again, and hear again the sound of that voice! I have haunted this place, these gardens – for many, many nights – with a faint, very faint hope of seeing you. This was the only chance that remained for me; and, thank Heaven! it has at length succeeded – I am not condemned to absolute despair!'

The Mysteries of Udolpho, ANN RADCLIFF 1764–1823

ow!

Out of your whole life give but a moment!
    All of your life that has gone before,
    All to come after it, – so you ignore,
So you make perfect the present; condense,
In a rapture of rage, for perfection's endowment,
Thought and feeling and soul and sense,
Merged in a moment which gives me at last
You around me for once, you beneath me, above me –
Me, sure that, despite of time future, time past,
This tick of life-time's one moment you love me!
How long such suspension may linger? Ah, Sweet,
    The moment eternal – just that and no more –
    When ecstasy's utmost we clutch at the core,
While cheeks burn, arms open, eyes shut, and lips meet!

ROBERT BROWNING 1812–89

THE PITY OF LOVE

A pity beyond all telling
Is hid in the heart of love:
The folk who are buying and selling,
The clouds on their journey above,
The cold wet winds ever blowing,
And the shadowy hazel grove
Where mouse-grey waters are flowing,
Threaten the head that I love.

WILLIAM BUTLER YEATS 1865-1939

# THE SUITOR

'You accept my devotion?' said Grandcourt, holding his hat by his side and looking straight into her eyes, without other movement. Their eyes meeting in that way seemed to allow any length of pause; but wait as long as she would, how could she contradict herself? What had she detained him for? He had shut out any explanation.

'Yes,' came as gravely from Gwendolen's lips as if she had been answering to her name in a court of justice. He received it gravely, and they still looked at each other in the same attitude.

Was there ever before such a way of accepting the bliss-giving 'Yes'? Grandcourt liked better to be at that distance from her, and to feel under a ceremony imposed by an indefinable prohibition that breathed from Gwendolen's bearing.

But he did at length lay down his hat and advance to take her hand, just pressing his lips upon it and letting it go again. She thought his behaviour perfect, and gained a sense of freedom which made her almost ready to be mischievous.

'Have you anything else to say to me?' said Gwendolen, playfully.

'Yes. – I know having things said to you is a great bore,' said Grandcourt, rather sympathetically.

'Not when they are things I like to hear.'

'Will it bother you to be asked how soon we can be married?'

'I think it will, to-day,' said Gwendolen, putting up her chin saucily.

'Not to-day, then, but to-morrow. Think of it before I come morrow. In a fortnight – or three weeks – as soon as possible.'

Daniel Deronda, GEORGE ELIOT 1819–80

[49]

$\mathcal{I}$F LOVE

If love were what the rose is,
  And I were like the leaf,
Our lives would grow together
In sad or singing weather,
Blown fields or flowerful closes,
  Green pleasure or grey grief;
If love were what the rose is,
  And I were like the leaf.

ALGERNON CHARLES SWINBURNE 1837–1909

WHEN TO HER LUTE

When to her lute Corinna sings,
Her voice revives the leaden strings,
And doth in highest notes appear
As any challenged echo clear.
But when she doth of mourning speak,
E'en with her sighs the strings do break.

And as her lute doth live or die,
Led by her passion, so must I.
For when of pleasure she doth sing,
My thoughts enjoy a sudden spring;
But if she doth of sorrow speak,
E'en from my heart the strings do break.

THOMAS CAMPION 1567–1619

KATE

I know her by her angry air,
Her bright-black eyes, her bright-black hair,
   Her rapid laughters wild and shrill,
As laughter of the woodpecker
   From the bosom of a hill.
   'Tis Kate – she sayeth what she will:
For Kate hath an unbridled tongue,
   Clear as the twanging of a harp.
     Her heart is like a throbbing star.
Kate hath a spirit ever strung
   Like a new bow, and bright and sharp
     As edges of the scymetar.
Whence shall she take a fitting mate?
   For Kate no common love will feel;
My woman-soldier, gallant Kate,
   As pure and true as blades of steel.

ALFRED, LORD TENNYSON 1809–92

ARE THEY THINE EYES THAT SHINE

And is it night? Are they thine eyes that shine?
    Are we alone and here and here alone?
May I come near, may I but touch thy shrine?
    Is Jealousy asleep, and is he gone?
O Gods, no more, silence my lips with thine,
    Lips, kisses, joys, hap, blessings most divine.

O come, my dear, our griefs are turn'd to night,
    And night to joys, night blinds pale Envy's eyes,
Silence and sleep prepare us our delight,
    O cease we then our woes, our griefs, our cries,
O vanish words, words do but passions move,
    O dearest life, joys sweet, O sweetest love.

ANONYMOUS SEVENTEENTH CENTURY

An ABSENT LOVER RETURNS

Molly was sitting in her pretty white invalid's dress, half reading, half dreaming, for the June air was so clear and ambient, the garden so full of bloom, the trees so full of leaf, that reading by the open window was only a pretence at such a time; besides which, Mrs Gibson continually interrupted her with remarks about the pattern of her worsted work. It was after lunch – orthodox calling time, when Maria ushered in Mr Roger Hamley. Molly started up; and then stood shyly and quietly in her place while a bronzed, bearded, grave man came into the room, in whom she at first had to seek for the merry boyish face she knew by heart only two years ago. But months in the climates in which Roger had been travelling age as much as years in more temperate regions. And constant thought and anxiety, while in daily peril of life, deepen the lines of character upon the face. Moreover, the circumstances that had of late affected him personally were not of a nature to make him either buoyant or cheerful. But his voice was the same; that was the first point of the old friend Molly caught, when he addressed her in a tone far softer than he used in speaking conventional politeness to her step-mother.

'I was so sorry to hear how ill you had been! You are looking but delicate!' letting his eyes rest upon her face with affectionate examination. Molly felt herself colour all over with the consciousness of his regard. To do something to put an end to it, she looked up, and showed him her beautiful soft grey eyes, which he never remembered to have noticed before.

Wives and Daughters, ELIZABETH GASKELL 1812–65

CHLOE IS MY REAL FLAME

The merchant, to secure his treasure,
    Conveys it in a borrow'd name:
Euphelia serves to grace my measure;
    But Chloe is my real flame.

MATTHEW PRIOR 1664–1721

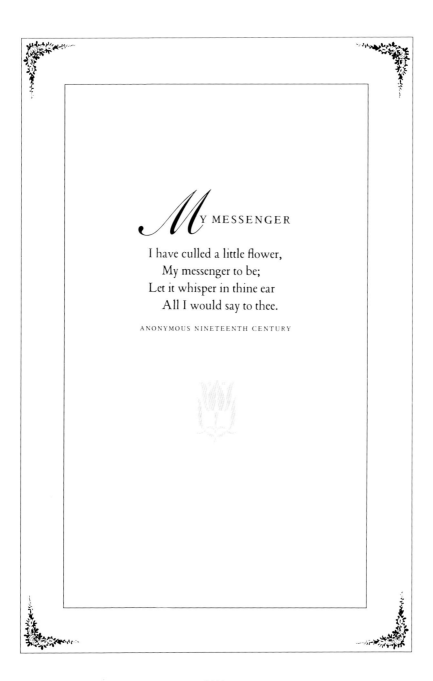

$\mathcal{M}$Y MESSENGER

I have culled a little flower,
My messenger to be;
Let it whisper in thine ear
All I would say to thee.

ANONYMOUS NINETEENTH CENTURY

KNOW YOU FAIR

Know you, fair, on what you look;
Divinest love lies in this book:
Expecting fire from your eyes,
To kindle this his sacrifice.
When your hands untie these strings,
Think you have an angel by th' wings.
One that gladly will be nigh,
To wait upon each morning sigh.
To flutter in the balmy air
Of your well-perfumèd prayer.

RICHARD CRASHAW 1613?–49

 PRING BEGINS

For winter's rains and ruins are over,
    And all the season of snows and sins;
The days dividing lover and lover,
    The light that loses, the night that wins;
And time remembered is grief forgotten,
And frosts are slain and flowers begotten,
And in green underwood and cover
    Blossom by blossom the spring begins.

ALGERNON CHARLES SWINBURNE 1837–1909

WILL YOU WEAR MY FAVOUR

He look'd, and more amazed
 Than if seven men had set upon him, saw
The maiden standing in the dewy light.
 He had not dream'd she was so beautiful.
Then came on him a sort of sacred fear,
 For silent, tho' he greeted her, she stood
Rapt on his face as if it were a God's.
 Suddenly flash'd on her a wild desire,
That he should wear her favour at the tilt.
 She braved a riotous heart in asking for it.
'Fair lord, whose name I know not – noble it is,
 I well believe, the noblest – will you wear
My favour at this tourney?' 'Nay,' said he,
 'Fair lady, since I never yet have worn
Favour of any lady in the lists.
 Such is my wont, as those who know me, know.'
'Yea, so,' she answer'd; 'then in wearing mine
 Needs must be lesser likelihood, noble lord,
That those who know should know you.' And he turn'd
 Her counsel up and down within his mind,
And found it true, and answer'd, 'True, my child.
 Well, I will wear it: fetch it out to me:
What is it?' and she told him 'A red sleeve
 Broider'd with pearls,' and brought it: then he bound
Her token on his helmet, with a smile,
 Saying, 'I never yet have done so much
For any maiden living,' and the blood
 Sprang to her face and fill'd her with delight.

Idylls of the King, ALFRED, LORD TENNYSON 1809–92

*Y*OUR BEAUTIFUL FLOWERS

... Your beautiful flowers! – none the less beautiful for waiting for water yesterday. As fresh as ever, they were; and while I was putting them into the water, I thought that your visit went on all the time. Other thoughts too I had, which made me look down blindly, quite blindly, on the little blue flowers ... while I thought what I could not have said an hour before without breaking into tears which would have run faster then. To say now that I never can forget, – that I feel myself bound to you as one human being cannot be more bound to another; – and that you are more to me at this moment than all the rest of the world, – is only to say in new words that it would be a wrong against *myself*, to seem to risk your happiness and abuse your generosity. For *me* ... though you threw out words yesterday about the testimony of a 'third person', it would be monstrous to assume it to be necessary to vindicate my trust of you – *I trust you implicitly* – and let us wait and see what this winter does or undoes – while God does His part for good, as we know – I will never fail to you from any human influence whatever – *that* I have promised – but you must let it be different from the other sort of promise which it would be a wrong to make. May God bless you – you, whose fault it is, to be too generous. You *are* not like other men, as I could see from the beginning – no –

Shall I have the proof tonight, I ask myself.

ELIZABETH BARRETT BROWNING 1806–61

HE SEA

Love still has something of the sea,
From whence his mother rose;
No time his slaves from doubt can free,
Nor give their thoughts repose:

They are becalmed in clearest days,
   And in rough weather tost;
They wither under cold delays,
   Or are in tempests lost.

One while they seem to touch the port,
   Then straight into the main,
Some angry wind in cruel sport
   The vessel drives again.

At first disdain and pride they fear,
   Which if they chance to 'scape,
Rivals and falsehood soon appear
   In a more dreadful shape.

By such degrees to Joy they come,
   And are so long withstood,
So slowly they receive the sum,
   It hardly does them good.

'Tis cruel to prolong a pain,
   And to defer a joy,
Believe me, gentle Celemene,
   Offends the wingèd Boy.

An hundred thousand oaths your fears
   Perhaps would not remove;
And if I gazed a thousand years
   I could no deeper love.

SIR CHARLES SEDLEY 1639–1701

*L*OVE IS ENOUGH

Love is enough: though the World be a-waning,
And the woods have no voice but the voice of complaining,
   Though the skies be too dark for dim eyes to discover
The gold-cups and daisies fair blooming thereunder,
Though the hills be held shadows, and the sea a dark wonder,
   And this day draw a veil over all deeds pass'd over,
Yet their hands shall not tremble, their feet shall not falter:
The void shall not weary, the fear shall not alter
   These lips and these eyes of the loved and the lover.

WILLIAM MORRIS 1834–96

NEW LOVE, NEW LIFE

She, who so long has lain
   Stone-stiff with folded wings,
Within my heart again
   The brown bird wakes and sings.

Brown nightingale, whose strain
   Is heard by day, by night,
She sings of joy and pain,
   Of sorrow and delight.

'Tis true, – in other days
   Have I unbarred the door;
He knows the walks and ways –
   Love has been here before.

Love blest and love accurst
   Was here in days long past;
This time is not the first,
   But this time is the last.

AMY LEVY 1861–89

*S*WEET WILLIAM'S FAREWELL TO BLACK-EYED SUSAN

All in the Downs the fleet was moored,
　The streamers waving in the wind,
When black-eyed Susan came aboard,
　　'Oh! where shall I my true love find?
Tell me, ye jovial sailors, tell me true,
If my sweet William sails among the crew.'

William, who high upon the yard,
　Rocked with the billow to and fro,
Soon as her well-known voice he heard,
　　He sighed, and cast his eyes below:
The cord slides swiftly through his glowing hands
And, quick as lightning, on the deck he stands.

'O Susan, Susan, lovely dear,
    My vows shall ever true remain;
Let me kiss off that falling tear,,
    We only part to meet again.
Change, as ye list, ye winds; my heart shall be
The faithful compass that still points to thee.

Believe not what the landsmen say,
    Who tempt with doubts thy constant mind:
They'll tell thee, sailors, when away,
    In every port a mistress find.
Yes, yes, believe them when they tell thee so,
For thou art present whereso'er I go.

Though battle call me from thy arms,
    Let not my pretty Susan mourn;
Though cannons roar, yet safe from harms,
    William shall to his dear return.
Love turns aside the balls that round me fly,
Lest precious tears should drop from Susan's eye.'

The boatswain gave the dreadful word,
    The sails their swelling bosom spread,
No longer must she stay aboard:
    They kissed, she sighed, he hung his head.
Her lessening boat unwilling rows to land:
'Adieu,' she cries, and waved her lily hand.

JOHN GAY 1685–1732

[75]

AND THEN I WAS IN LOVE

Once did my thoughts both ebb and flow,
   As passion did them move;
Once did I hope, straight fear again –
   And then I was in love.

Once did I waking spend the night,
   And told how many minutes move;
Once did I wishing waste the day –
   And then I was in love.

Once, by my carving true love's knot,
   The weeping trees did prove
That wounds and tears were both our lot –
   And then I was in love.

ANONYMOUS SEVENTEENTH CENTURY

ℒOVERS

In a moment the figure was in his arms, and his lips upon hers.

'My Eustacia!'

'Clym, dearest!'

Such a situation had less than three months brought forth.

They remained long without a single utterance for no language could reach the level of their condition: words were as the rusty implements of a by-gone barbarous epoch, and only to be occasionally tolerated.

'I began to wonder why you did not come,' said Yeobright, when she had withdrawn a little from his embrace.

'You said ten minutes after the first mark of shade on the edge of the moon; and that's what it is now.'

'Well, let us only think that here we are.'

Then, holding each other's hand, they were again silent, and the shadow on the moon's disc grew a little larger.

'Has it seemed long since you last saw me?' she asked.

'It has seemed sad.'

'And not long? That's because you occupy yourself, and so blind yourself to my absence. To me, who can do nothing, it has been like living under stagnant water.'

'I would rather bear tediousness, dear, than have time made short by such means as have shortened mine.'

'In what way is that? You have been thinking you wished you did not love me.'

'How can a man wish that, and yet love on? No, Eustacia.'

'Men can, women cannot.'

'Well, whatever I may have thought, one thing is certain – I do love you – past all compass and description. I love you to oppressiveness – I, who have never before felt more than a pleasant passing fancy for any woman I have ever seen. Let me look right into your moonlit face, and dwell on every line and curve in it! Only a few hair-breadths make the difference between this face and faces I have seen many times before I knew you; yet what a difference – the difference between everything and nothing at all. One touch on that mouth again! there, and there, and there.

The Return of the Native, THOMAS HARDY 1840-1928

$\mathscr{I}$N PRAISE OF TWO

Faustina hath the fairer face,
And Phillida the better grace,
   Both haue mine eye enriched.
This sings full sweetly with her voyce,
Her fingers make as sweet a noyse,
   Both haue mine eare bewitched:
Ay me! sith Fates haue so prouided,
My heart (alas) must be divided.

ANONYMOUS SEVENTEENTH CENTURY

$\mathcal{T}$HE LANGUAGE OF LOVE

She sought for [the book] in which Valancourt had been reading the day before, and hoped for the pleasure of retracing a page over which the eyes of a beloved friend had lately passed, of dwelling on the passages which he had admired, and of permitting them to speak to her in the language of his own mind, and to bring himself to her presence. On searching for the book she could find it nowhere, but in its stead perceived a volume of Petrarch's poems, that had belonged to Valancourt, whose name was written in it, and from which he had frequently read passages to her with all the pathetic expression that characterized the feelings of the author.

She hesitated in believing, what would have been sufficiently apparent to almost any other person, that he had purposely left this book instead of the one she had lost, and that love had prompted the exchange; but having opened it with impatient pleasure, and observed the lines of his pencil drawn along the various passages he had read aloud, and under others more descriptive of delicate tenderness than he had dared to trust his voice with, the conviction came at length to her mind.

For some moment she was conscious only of being beloved; then, the recollection of all the variations of tone and countenance with which he had recited these sonnets, and of the soul which spoke in their expression, pressed to her memory, and she wept over the memorial of his affection.

The Mysteries of Udolpho, ANN RADCLIFFE 1764–1823

*I*F EVER TWO WERE ONE

If ever two were one, then surely we.
If ever man were loved by wife, then thee;
If ever wife was happy in a man,
Compare with me, ye women, if you can.
I prize thy love more than whole mines of gold
Or all the riches that the East doth hold.
My love is such that rivers cannot quench,
Nor ought but love from thee, give recompense.
Thy love is such I can no way repay,
The heavens reward thee manifold, I pray.
Then while we live, in love let's so persevere
That when we live no more, we may live ever.

ANNE BRADSTREET 1612?–72

 URE LOVE

Long in secret I have sighed, –
   For you all others I've denied,
And if your heart I cannot gain,
   I ne'er will wed another swain.
Pray my love an answer send,
   And let it be in honour penn'd,
That I may no longer languish,
   And soon, oh soon relieve my anguish.

ANONYMOUS NINETEENTH CENTURY

BIRTH OF LOVE

Love – it is the gift of Heaven,
Like the rose, how sweet its bloom,
And where'er is felt its presence,
There it dissipates each gloom.
And the heart that loveth truly,
In its first affection pure,
Shall, as long as life continues,
Find its happiness endure.

ANONYMOUS NINETEENTH CENTURY

UNDER THE WILLOW-SHADES

Under the willow-shades they were
   Free from the eye-sight of the sun,
For no intruding beam could there
   Peep through to spy what things were done:
     Thus sheltered they unseen did lie,
     Surfeiting on each other's eye;
Defended by the willow-shades alone,
The sun's heat they defied and cooled their own.

Whilst they did embrace unspied,
   The conscious willow seemed to smile,
That them with privacy supplied,
   Holding the door, as 't were, the while;
     And when their dalliances were o'er,
     The willows, to oblige them more,
Bowing, did seem to say, as they withdrew,
'We can supply you with a cradle too.'

WILLIAM DAVENANT 1606–68

$\mathcal{S}$UCH A LOVE AS YOU

My sweet Girl,

Your Letter gave me more delight, than any thing in the world but yourself could do; indeed I am almost astonished that any absent one should have that luxurious power over my senses which I feel. Even when I am not thinking of you I receive your influence and a tenderer nature steeling upon me. All my thoughts, my unhappiest days and nights have I find not at all cured me of my love of Beauty, but made it so intense that I am miserable that you are not with me: or rather breathe in that dull sort of patience that cannot be called Life. I never knew before, what such a love as you have made me feel, was; I did not believe in it; my Fancy was affraid of it, lest it should burn me up. You say you are affraid I shall think you do not love me — in saying this you make me ache the more to be near you. I am at the diligent use of my faculties here, I do not pass a day without sprawling some blank verse or tagging some rhymes; and here I must confess, that, (since I am on that subject,) I love you the more in that I believe you have liked me for my own sake and for nothing else.

Letter to Fanny Bawne, JOHN KEATS 1795–1821

HE FAN

For various purpose serves the fan,
    As thus – a decent blind,
Between the sticks to peep at man,
    Nor yet betray your mind.

Each action has a meaning plain:
    Resentment's in the snap;
A flirt expresses strong disdain,
    Consent a tiny tap.

All passions will the fan disclose,
    All modes of female art;
And to advantage sweetly shows
    The hand if not the heart.

'Tis Folly's sceptre, first designed
    By Love's capricious boy,
Who knows how lightly all mankind
    Are governed by a toy.

ROBERT LLOYD 1733–64

ACKNOWLEDGEMENTS

The publishers wish to thank the following for permission to reproduce the illustrations: Bridgeman Art Library, London, with acknowledgements to: Roy Miles Fine Paintings, London: Slipcase and Frontispiece; Brooklyn Museum, New York, p. 9; Christopher Wood Gallery, London pp. 10–11; Guildhall Art Gallery, London pp. 16, 73, 74; Private Collections pp. 27, 90; Bury Art Gallery, Lancashire p. 30; Towneley Hall Art Gallery and Museum, Burnley p. 33; Fine Lines (Fine Art) Warwickshire p. 48; Glasgow City Art Gallery and Museum p. 55; Connaught Brown, London p. 86; Nardoni Galerie, Prague p. 89. Bury Street Gallery, London pp. 29, 82. Christie's Colour Library, London pp. 20–21, 44, 56, 65, 93. Mary Evans Picture Library, London p. 4. Fine Art Photographic Library, London pp. 13, 14, 15, 22, 32, 35, 40, 43, 50, 51, 52, 60, 62, 63, 68, 70–71, 78, 85. Hancocks and Co (Jewellers) Ltd., London: Miniature Frame on Slipcase and Cover. Julian Hartnell, London p. 44. Manchester City Art Gallery p. 25. Photographs by courtesy of David Messum Fine Paintings, London WI pp. 6–7, 67. Reproduced by permission of the Trustees of The Wallace Collection, London p. 77. Photographs by courtesy of Christopher Wood Gallery, London p. 39.

LIST OF PAINTINGS